TONY BENNETT
A Little Golden Book® Biography

By Deborah Hopkinson
Illustrated by Barbara Bongini

The editors would like to thank Scott Simon, journalist, author, and host of NPR's *Weekend Edition Saturday,* for his assistance in the preparation of this book.

A GOLDEN BOOK • NEW YORK

Text copyright © 2023 by Deborah Hopkinson
Cover art and interior illustrations copyright © 2023 by Barbara Bongini
All rights reserved. Published in the United States by Golden Books, an imprint of Random House Children's Books, a division of Penguin Random House LLC, 1745 Broadway, New York, NY 10019. Golden Books, A Golden Book, A Little Golden Book, the G colophon, and the distinctive gold spine are registered trademarks of Penguin Random House LLC.
rhcbooks.com
Educators and librarians, for a variety of teaching tools, visit us at
RHTeachersLibrarians.com
Library of Congress Control Number: 2022941219
ISBN 978-0-593-64510-9 (trade) — ISBN 978-0-593-64511-6 (ebook)
Printed in the United States of America
10 9 8 7 6 5 4 3 2 1

Tony Bennett was born Anthony Dominick Benedetto on August 3, 1926, in New York City. His grandparents had been poor farmers in southern Italy. Like many immigrants, Tony's family came to America for a better life.

Tony and his older siblings, Mary and John, lived with their parents in a small apartment in Astoria, a neighborhood in the borough of Queens. For a long time, their only heat came from a coal-burning stove in the kitchen.

Tony and John slept in the back room. Some nights were very cold. *Brrr!*

The Benedettos all worked hard, but Sundays were just for family. Everyone gathered at Tony's grandparents' house. After a delicious meal, Tony, Mary, and John sang and told jokes while their uncles played music. Tony and John had beautiful voices, just like their dad.

When Tony's dad was a small boy in Italy, he would sing from a nearby mountaintop so the whole village could hear.

Tony felt lucky to have a loving family. He had teachers who helped him, too. One arranged for Tony to sing at the grand opening of the Triborough Bridge in 1936.

What a spectacular day! Nine-year-old Tony and Mayor La Guardia led the crowd in song as they marched over the new bridge. Tony's heart was full. He knew he wanted to keep singing to make people happy.

It wasn't always easy for Tony to be happy, though. His father died when Tony was ten. Tony missed him a lot. His dad was gentle and kind and taught him to respect others.

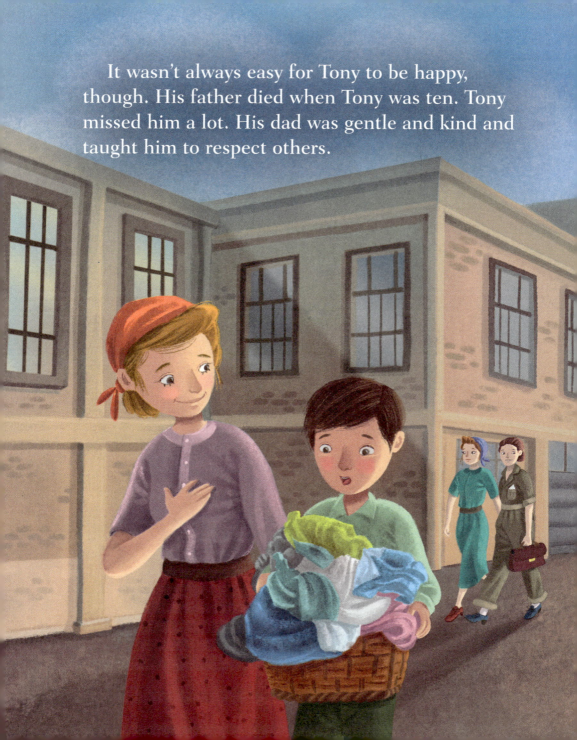

It was the Great Depression, when times were hard everywhere. To support the family, Tony's mom worked in a garment factory. Tony waited at the subway to help her carry a bundle of dresses home to sew at night for extra money.

Even when she was tired, Tony's mom made sure to do excellent work. Tony decided he would always do his best, too, to make his mother proud and honor his father's memory.

Along with singing, Tony loved to paint and draw. His art teacher at school saw his talent and gave him extra lessons.

Tony was accepted into a new high school for artists. Today it's called the High School of Art and Design. But he wasn't able to finish. To help his family, Tony had to leave school and get a job. He became a singing waiter.

When he turned eighteen, Tony was drafted into the army during World War II. In the winter of 1945, he was sent to fight in Germany. Once, Tony woke up covered in snow! But even while shivering in the trenches, he made art, sketching pictures whenever he could.

After peace came, Tony stayed in Germany a while longer. He joined a military band, singing to cheer up American troops.

On Thanksgiving Day in 1945, Tony ran into Frank Smith, a friend from high school. Tony invited Frank to come to a special holiday dinner for American soldiers still in Germany.

But when the friends arrived, an officer wouldn't let them in. He yelled and tore the corporal stripes off Tony's uniform, making him a lower-rank private again.

Why? The army didn't treat Black soldiers and white soldiers equally. Although Frank and other African Americans risked their lives to serve their country, they weren't allowed to eat with white soldiers. This was called segregation. Tony knew it was wrong, and he would never forget what happened that day.

Along with losing his rank, Tony was fired from the band. Luckily, another officer heard of a new army band being formed and helped Tony get in. This time, Tony performed on the radio. Soldiers all over Germany tuned in to listen.

Tony loved it! When he returned to New York in 1946, he was eager to become a professional singer.

Tony knocked on many doors. He auditioned for many singing jobs. Sometimes he sang for free. No matter how hard it got, Tony kept trying.

A few years later, Tony had his first big break. The great Pearl Bailey heard him sing at a club called the Greenwich Village Inn. When Pearl was asked to be the main act, she agreed—but only if Tony was hired, too.

One night, Bob Hope came to the show. He was so impressed, he invited Tony to sing with him at the famous Paramount Theater!

Bob also gave Tony the stage name that we know him by: Tony Bennett.

Tony's glorious adventure had begun. Tony's first album came out soon after, in 1952. The title song, "Because of You," became a huge hit. Almost overnight, Tony was a star.

Tony's rich, velvety voice touched people's hearts. His energy, enthusiasm, and smile lifted their spirits.

Tony Bennett made people happy—and he's been doing it ever since.

Around the time Tony's career took off, he was also lucky in love. He married and started a family. Tony has two sons, Dae and Danny, and two daughters, Joanna and Antonia. Antonia is a singer, too.

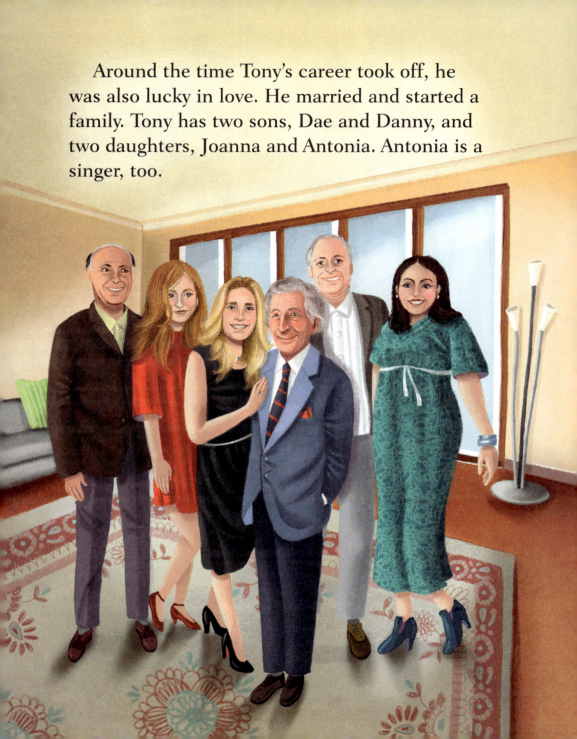

Tony married his third wife, Susan Crow, in 2007. Together they began Exploring the Arts, a program to strengthen the arts in high schools to help young people achieve their dreams.

"Giving back is one of the best things that anyone can do."

Tony has always loved making music with others. During the 1960s, he often performed with Black musicians, including Nat King Cole and Duke Ellington. But America was still segregated. Even famous people were turned away from hotels and restaurants because of the color of their skin.

Tony knew it was time for him to take a stand for justice and equality. In 1965, he joined Reverend Martin Luther King Jr. for an important civil rights march in Selma, Alabama.

Celebrities like Tony, Harry Belafonte, and Sammy Davis Jr. marched alongside brave activists like John Lewis. Afterward, Tony and other singers performed for the marchers on a makeshift stage.

Tony has sung for eleven presidents. Many of his songs are considered American classics, such as "The Way You Look Tonight," "Fly Me to the Moon," and "I Left My Heart in San Francisco."

Tony is a singing legend, but he has never stopped painting. Some of his pieces hang in museums. Tony has always signed his art with "Benedetto," his family name, which means "blessed" in Italian.

Tony feels blessed that he has been able to perform for so long. At age eighty, he began a project called *Duets*, singing popular songs with other stars. In 2021, when his second album with Lady Gaga came out, he was ninety-five—the oldest person ever to release an album of new songs!

In his eighties, Tony visited the mountaintop in Italy where his father had stood so many years before. Tony sang "O Solo Mio," filling the valley with beautiful music.

Coming to America was a dream for Tony's family. And his family's love and encouragement helped Tony bring his own dreams to life.

Tony Bennett's voice will always touch our hearts and remind us to smile.